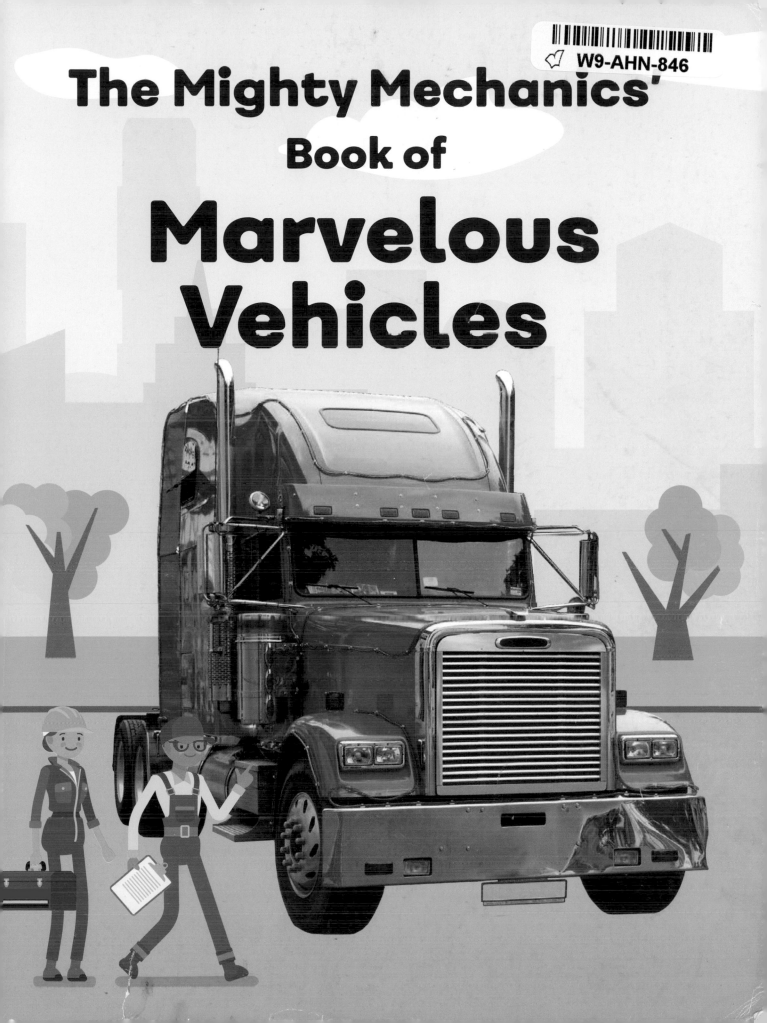

The Mighty Mechanics'
Book of
Marvelous Vehicles

Design: Perfect Bound Ltd

Beetle Books and Hungry Banana are imprints of Hungry Tomato

First published in Great Britain in 2020 by Hungry Tomato Ltd
F1, Old Bakery Studios,
Malpas Road, Truro,
Cornwall, TR1 1QH, UK

Copyright © 2020 Hungry Tomato Ltd

A CIP catalogue record for this book is available from the British Library

US edition (Beetle Books)
ISBN 978-1-913077-76-1

UK edition (Hungry Banana)
ISBN 978-1-913077-31-0

Printed and bound in China

Discover more at
www.mybeetlebooks.com
www.hungrytomato.com

Contents

The Mighty Mechanics

We sometimes use a **mallet** to break parts off a vehicle

Pliers can grip round items

We are the Mighty Mechanics.
Welcome to our **workshop!** We
work on some amazing vehicles.
Here are a few of the **tools** we use
to fix them.

This is a
hacksaw,
used for cutting
through thin
pieces of metal

We will need a large **wrench**
for undoing large bolts

Tractor

Tractors do many jobs on a farm. They work in the sunshine, snow, and rain.

This tractor is lifting a heavy bale of straw

Mirrors allow the driver to see behind them

The **cab** is where the driver sits

Tractors have tough, thick wheels to grip in muddy fields

Tractors have small wheels at the front to help them turn around in small circles

Tractor and Plow

This **tractor** is pulling a **plow** to dig up the earth. Then the farmer can **SOW** seed into the ground for plants to grow.

The **blades** pulled by this tractor are digging **furrows**

This is called a moldboard. It turns the earth over

Metal blades called coulters cut straight down into the ground

Combine Harvester

A **combine harvester** does two jobs at once. First, it cuts up and gathers the crops. Then it separates the grain from the rest of the plant.

Straw is pushed out of the combine harvester

740

A combine harvester cuts and pulls in the crop

When the tank is full, the grain is emptied into a **trailer**

Inside, a spinning **drum** shakes the grains off the plant

These spikes push the cut crops into the combine harvester

A blade cuts off the bottom of the plant

Garbage Truck

Garbage trucks collect the trash from our homes. They keep our cities and neighborhoods clean.

This is a
rear loader
garbage truck

Garbage trucks pick up trash in the early morning in the city

These controls operate the machinery

The trash is placed in the back of the truck, where it is crushed

When this machine is switched on, the trash is tipped out of the Truck

13

Big Rig Truck

A **big rig truck** has a powerful **engine** to pull heavy trailers. It can travel hundreds and thousands of miles to deliver its goods.

A big rig truck has a very loud horn

Smelly fumes are blown out of the **exhaust**

Trailers are added to big rigs to haul heavy goods

Some cabs are so big, the driver can sleep in them

Big rig trucks use lots of gas, so they need big gas tanks

Tanker

This **tanker** is carrying gas to power our vehicles or heat our homes. Tankers can carry powders and gasses as well as liquids.

Gas can be dangerous, so tanker drivers are trained to drive very carefully

Tankers have warning signs on them to show what's inside

Tankers have curved sides, which are stronger than flat ones

At the gas station, the gas is poured into big underground tanks

Monster Truck

This incredible machine is a **pick-up truck**. It has been built to race over bumpy and muddy courses. It is raised high, so it can drive over anything in its way.

The power from the engine goes to all four wheels

Each wheel is larger than a person

This wheel will be fitted to a monster truck

These are giant **shock absorbers,** which act like cushions as they go over bumps

Lowboy

A **lowboy** has a trailer that is low to the ground. This makes it easier to get heavy loads on and off. This one has a large **dumper** on it.

This dumper is wider than the trailer. A separate car with flashing lights may drive in front of the lowboy to warn other vehicles

This trailer has lots of wheels to help carry the heavy load

This **excavating** machine is being driven off the trailer to start work

Cables carry power to the lowboy's brakes and lights

21

Tow Truck

A **tow truck** is used when a vehicle breaks down or has an accident. The tow truck can lift the car out of trouble and tow it away.

This cab has broken down and is being taken to a garage for repairs

This cable is made of metal wire and is very strong

This large arm is called the boom

A big hook is used to lift vehicles that need rescuing

Tools are kept in **compartments** at the side

Excavators

There are lots of different types of **excavators** and they come in all sizes. They are mainly used for digging. This one is called a **backhoe**.

The **ram** slides in and out to move the excavator's arm

For small holes and ditches, you need a mini excavator

This long arm is known as the boom

This is called the **dipper**, because it dips in and out of the ground

These metal teeth make it easier to cut through the earth

Dump Truck

Dump trucks can carry large loads and lift up so that the loads slide out. Some small dump trucks are called tipper trucks.

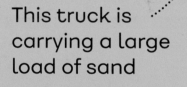

This truck is carrying a large load of sand

The top board protects the cab from falling rocks

This tipper's long ram lifts the body very high to empty the whole load

This dump truck has 10 wheels and a spare tire on the side

Concrete Mixer

This truck makes and delivers **concrete** to building sites. Sand, gravel, water, and **cement** are mixed together to make the concrete.

This is the water tank ······>

Concrete pours out of the metal tube at the rear of the truck

The drum turns about eight times a minute

The cement, gravel, and sand are poured in here

29

Crawler Excavator

Large **excavators** that have tracks instead of wheels are called *"crawlers"*. The tracks help the excavator grip on muddy ground.

Radio antenna

You have to climb up a ladder to get into the cab

Seat for the driver

These large excavators are used for big jobs such as **demolition**, mining, and building roads

This large bucket can move more than 500 shovelfuls of earth at a time

31

Road Roller

Every new road needs a **roller** to make sure the surface is flat. The road roller flattens the road with its heavy metal rollers.

The rear wheels have tires on them—and some have rollers at the back as well

The roller has flattened some of the road, but the rest of the road is still rough

A roller weighs the same as 18 cars

The roller can be filled with sand or water to make it heavier

Pneumatic Drill

This excavator has a large **drill** on the end of its arm. It is used mainly for breaking up concrete.

This drill breaks concrete into smaller lumps that can then be removed easily

Smaller pieces of concrete are broken up with a smaller **pneumatic** hammer

This is the control that operates the drill

The excavator has stabilizers to keep it still as the arm goes up and down

35

Bulldozer

Bulldozers push tree stumps, earth, and stones out of the way with a huge metal blade. They are clearing the ground ready for building. This is called **dozing**.

This dozer is for very heavy work and has tracks to help it move over muddy ground

The blade is curved to help move the earth away

Headlamps help the driver to see in bad weather and in the dark

This metal arm is called a tilt ram. It lifts the blade

Paver

A **paver** spreads a layer of **asphalt** on the road. Asphalt is a mixture of hot tar and small stones. It is the top surface layer of most roads.

As the paver drives along, the asphalt comes out from the back

As the warm asphalt comes out, a metal plate spreads it into a thin layer

First, a **grader** smoothes a flat layer of stones over the ground. Then the paver lays the asphalt

The front of the paver is called a **hopper** and is where the asphalt is stored

The asphalt sets hard as it cools

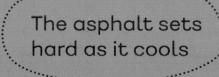

Hydraulic Drilling Machine

Hydraulic drilling machines are used to drill giant holes at construction sites. The drill at the front is called an **auger.**

On the side of the boom is a ladder, in case the operator needs to climb to the top. It's a long way up!

This construction site has three drilling machines digging holes for the **foundations** of a new building

The driver sits in the cab at the bottom

This collar holds the auger still as it drills into the ground

This arm tilts the auger so it can drill straight into the ground or at an angle

Ambulance

Ambulances carry sick or injured people to hospital in **emergencies**. Ambulances have a lot of equipment to keep people alive. They even have tools to help deliver babies.

Ambulances have loud sirens and flashing lights to tell other people to "get out the way" when they are driving to an emergency

Each ambulance has a **two-way radio** to update the hospital on the condition of the patient

Ambulances have highly trained **emergency medical technicians (EMTs)** to look after sick and injured people

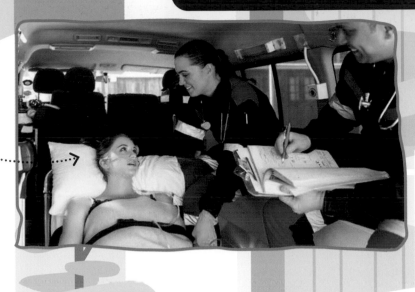

AMBULANCE

Ambulances are usually called by phone on a special emergency number.

At the back of the ambulance is a **tail-lift** to help lift patients in and out

43

Fire Truck

These **fire trucks** rush firefighters to the fire. They have all the equipment they need to **fight fires** and rescue people. A fire truck like this can carry up to eight firefighters.

Inside each truck is a tank to carry water for putting out the flames

This fire truck is putting out a fire at the side of the road

Water is sprayed on fires through hoses. When they are not being used, the hoses are squashed flat and stored here

Ladders are used to rescue people and sometimes animals

A hose is attached to the water tank at this valve

Search and Rescue Helicopter

This is the **MH-65 Dolphin**—a search and rescue **helicopter**. It has two pilots, a flight mechanic, and a rescue swimmer.

These **rotor** blades lift the helicopter into the air. It can fly at up to 200 miles per hour (320 kph)

These wheels are pulled up into the helicopter after it has taken off

A rescue swimmer is jumping out of the helicopter to rescue someone in the water

It has two very powerful engines

6551

NORTH BEND

DANGER

KEEP AWAY

COAST GUARD

EXHAUST

This small rotor is used to control the helicopter's direction when it is flying

Fireboat

Fireboats are used to **fight fires** on ships and buildings that are close to the water. They have large pumps to spray water onto the fires. Fireboats draw the water from the sea around them.

Fireboats sometimes shoot water in the air to welcome historical or naval ships

A fireboat may carry doctors and EMTs to an emergency

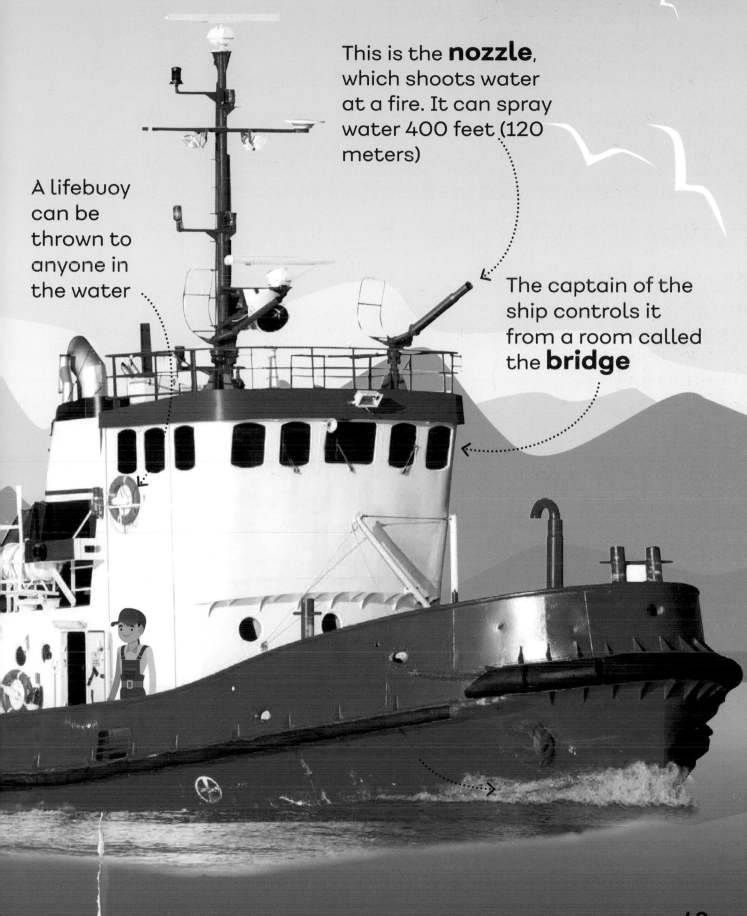

This is the **nozzle**, which shoots water at a fire. It can spray water 400 feet (120 meters)

A lifebuoy can be thrown to anyone in the water

The captain of the ship controls it from a room called the **bridge**

Police Car

Police cars are used for **patrolling** or responding to **crimes**. They have distinctive colors so people can identify them. Police cars can chase fleeing criminals at high speed.

Police cars can drive over 130 miles per hour (200 kph)

13

On the roof are flashing lights and a loud siren to warn people the police are coming

This police officer is using an in-car computer. It can be used for contacting the police station

POLICE

TO PROTECT AND SERVE

EMERGENCY
911

This car has extra strong sides to protect the officers inside

51

Airport Crash Tender

An **airport crash tender** is a special truck for fighting fires at airports. They are usually very **BIG**.

They don't need long ladders, as aircraft are not as tall as large buildings

They have big wheels, which allow them to drive over wreckage

Crash tenders have powerful nozzles to spray foam onto burning planes. The foam **smothers** the fire

They carry LOTS of foam in tanks

Rescue Submersible

This is a **rescue submersible**. It saves sailors from submarines that are in trouble. It is carried to the rescue site by a **mother ship**.

This is where the sailor controls the submersible when it is at the surface

This submersible can rescue all the sailors from even the largest submarine

This submersible has just returned to the surface to be loaded back onto its mother ship

This round tube is where the submersible attaches to a submarine. The sailors can crawl through it to safety

Snowblower

When roads are blocked by snow, a **snowblower** will clear them. It collects the snow and **blows** it onto the side of the road.

Snow is sprayed up this chute and away from the road

As the truck moves along, it clears a path through the snow

Powerful headlights allow the driver to see in the dark

Blades on a drum at the front **churn** up the snow. As the drum spins, it flings the snow up out of the chute

It has two engines. One drives the truck and the other turns the drum

Chains stop the wheels slipping on the snow

Lifeboat

This is a **lifeboat** to rescue people at sea. It is designed to sail in all weathers, even **hurricanes**. It can roll over completely and still sail on.

This lifeboat is on patrol on the *Potomac River* in the USA.

This door will not let water in, even if the lifeboat is upside down

The lifeboat can be controlled at the top when the weather is clear

When the weather is bad, the crew stays inside and controls the ship from here

It has windshield wipers. These swish away rain and spray so the crew can see where the boat is going

Large Mobile Cranes

Truck cranes move around on wheels. They have one cab for controlling the crane and another one for driving the truck.

This crane is lifting a heavy concrete support

This is the crane cab

Metal legs called outriggers **stabilize** the crane

This is the boom. It can reach up to the top of a six-story building

Monster Tractor

Giant tractors work in the big fields of **North America**. They can work for up to 24 hours without stopping.

Some wheat fields in America are so big it takes an hour to drive from one end to the other

The eight wheels on these tractors stop them from sinking into muddy ground

Tractors often work at night. They need lights so their drivers can see where they are going

Each massive tire is 8 feet (2.5 meters) tall

Australian Road Train

These **monster trucks** are the kings of the road in **Australia**. They drive vast distances to deliver their **cargo**.

The powerful engine helps the truck haul heavy loads at fast speeds.

This road train is driving through a remote part of Australia

This truck is pulling three trailers

They can carry enough gas to drive 1,000 miles (1,600 kilometers) before refueling

65

Giant Mining Machines

This enormous machine is a **bucket wheel excavator.** It is used to dig for coal.

These cables lower the bucket wheel until it touches the ground

When the wheel turns, buckets scrape up the coal

The wheels can scrape up 40,000 buckets of coal in one day

The coal moves onto a moving track inside the arm

The excavator moves slowly on tracks

Giant Floating Crane

Some **cranes** float on water. They are used to work on **oil rigs** and build bridges over water.

This crane is lifting part of a new ship into the water

Floating cranes use strong cables to lift huge ships out of the water

People sleep, eat, and work on these cranes for days at a time

NASA Crawler-transporter

This is the largest **transporter** in the world. It carries rockets and spacecraft to their launchpads.

Crawler-transporters move more slowly than a person walks when carrying a load

SIDE 3

SIDE

This crawler has carried a Space Shuttle spacecraft to its launchpad

The crawler has four tracks at each corner to drive it

BelAZ 75710 Monster Truck

This giant dump truck carries loads in mines. Its body can tilt so that the loads slide out.

The truck is too big to drive on normal roads

This truck can carry up to 440 tons (450 tonnes) of rocks

The driver has to climb this ladder to reach the cab

75710

The huge wheels are as tall as an adult

Dodge Power Wagon

This is the giant **Dodge Power Wagon**—the largest car in the world.

The windshield wipers are from a cruise ship

Inside, it has four bedrooms and a bathroom

The **tailgate** at the back can be lowered to make a viewing platform

The wheels are from an oil rig transporter

Antonov An-225 Plane

This is the **longest plane** in the world. It is 275 feet (84 meters) from nose to tail and also has the longest **wingspan**.

The Antonov holds the record for flying with the heaviest single load

The nose of the plane has been raised to load a helicopter

Six **jet engines** power the plane through the air

The plane lands and takes off on 32 wheels

Glossary

blades sharp cutting edges

boom a movable arm, as on a crane

bridge a room from where a boat is driven

cab the part of a vehicle where the driver sits

cargo goods carried by a large vehicle

cement building material made by mixing powder and water, which hardens when dry

churn stir violently

compartments storage spaces

demolition knocking down old buildings

dumper a truck with a tipping section that lifts to dump its contents

drum a cylindrical container

emergency medical technicians (EMTs) people who give medical help to sick or injured people on their way to hospital

engine a machine that uses energy to produce movement

excavating digging out and removing

excavator a heavy construction vehicle

exhaust a tube that carries dirty fumes away from the engine of a truck or tractor

foundations the underlying base of a building

furrows small ditches where seeds are planted

grader a machine for leveling earth

hurricane a very powerful storm

hydraulic machinery operated by pressurized oil or water

mining removal of coal or minerals from the ground

mother ship a ship serving a smaller craft

nozzle a device that directs and speeds up the flow of a liquid

oil rigs structures with equipment to remove oil from underground

patrolling driving around an area, looking out for criminals

pneumatic operated by air pressure

rear loader a truck that is loaded and unloaded at the back

rotor the spinning part of a helicopter or machine

smother put out by depriving of air

sow plant seed

stabilize to make steady

tailgate a gate at the rear of a vehicle that can be let down to form a flat surface

trailer a vehicle without an engine that can be pulled by another vehicle

wingspan the distance from the tip of one wing to the tip of the other

workshop a place where things are made or repaired

Index

Picture Credits

(abbreviations: t = top; b = bottom; m = middle; l = left; r = right; bg = background)

Alamy: AB Forces News Collection 55tr; Marmaduke St John 51tr. **NASA:** 70, 71tr. **Shutterstock:** Abscent 46bg; Alex Churilov 5m; Alex JW Robinson 77tr; Anastasiia Kozubenko 20bg, 36bg; Anastasiia Vasylyk 2bg, 28bg, 72bg; Anatoliy Lukich 47; Andrew Rybalko (all characters); AriSys 48bg, 68bg; Arthito 5 (pliers); Bannafarsai_Stock 40m; Bram van Broekhoven 48mr; Budimir Jevtic 39tr; Cezary Wojtkowski 64; chaphot 30; Charles Brutlag 9; Charles F McCarthy 47tr; Creativa Images 27; daseaford 59; David Touchtone 22; Dmitry Kalinovsky 31tr, 35; DniproDD 1bg, 12bg 34bg, 44bg, 70bg, 78bg; Dobresum 53; Douglas Litchfield 58ml; Droidworker 8bg, 10bg, 56bg, 62bg; Emrah AKYILDIZ 56ml; Eng. Bilal Izaddin 29tr; Eric Milos 67; ezp 6ml; Fotokostic 9tr; I'm friday 13; Igor Kovalchuk 5mr; Ihor Biliavsky 74bg; iur8 66bl; JIMMOYHT 52bg, 76bg; kamilpetran 76; Karin Hildebrand Lau 45tr; kemdim 73tr; Krivosheev Vitaly 10, 63; Laurens Hoddenbagh 62ml; LeitWolf 72; littleman 4ml; Louis.Roth 51; MadPixel 6bg; Mapleman13 32m, 33tr; Marquisphoto 17tr; MaryDesyv 30bg, 64bg, 66bg; MaryDesyv2 18bg; Mastak A 12bg, 38bg, 58bg; michaeljung 43tr; mojOjO 54bg; Nielskliim 13tr; Nigel Jarvis 19; Nightman1965 68; oksana.perkins 15tr; Oleksandr Derevianko 26bg, 40bg, 61bg, 68mr; Petr Studen 1; Philip Lange 75; photo-denver 23tr; Pro3DArt 37; ProStockStudio 22bg, 32bg, 42bg; Reinhard Tiburzy 21; rekandshoot 45; Rihardzz 17; Rob Wilson 26ml, 43; Roman023_ photography 21tr; SCK_Photo 57; Sergey Kohl 53tr; Sergey Logrus 36ml; sima 35tr; smereka 11tr; Smileus 41; StockPhotosArt 28; timothy passmore 15; tjades 61; tourpics_net 65tr; Tyler Olson8 49; Vectorpocket 4bg, 17bg, 24bg, 50bg; Vereshchagin Dmitry 24, 38; Vladimir Melnik 19tr. ZoranOrcik 60ml. **US Navy:** 54. www.hollandfoto.net: 24ml.